Jane Austen's Steventon

DEIRDRE LE FAYE

First Published in Great Britain 2007
by The Jane Austen Society
c/o Jane Austen's House, Chawton, Hampshire GU34 1SD

ISBN 978-0-9538174-9-8

Also by Deirdre Le Faye
A Chronology of Jane Austen and her Family 1600-2000
Jane Austen: A Family Record
Writers' Lives: Jane Austen
Jane Austen's 'Outlandish Cousin', the Life and Letters of Eliza de Feuillide
Jane Austen: the World of her Novels
The Jane Austen Cookbook (with Maggie Black)
So You Think You Know Jane Austen? (with John Sutherland)
Fanny Knight's Diaries: Jane Austen through her niece's eyes
and editor of
Jane Austen's Letters
Reminiscences of Jane Austen's Niece Caroline Austen

Printed by Sarsen Press, Hyde Street, Winchester, Hants

JANE AUSTEN'S STEVENTON

by Deirdre Le Faye

Take of English earth as much
As either hand may rightly clutch.
In the taking of it, breathe
Prayer for all who lie beneath -
Not the great nor well-bespoke
But the mere uncounted folk,
Of whose life and death is none
Report or lamentation.

From Rudyard Kipling, 'A Charm', 1910

The Jane Austen Society

CONTENTS

ACKNOWLEDGEMENTS

My most grateful thanks are due to:

The Revd Michael Kenning for writing the foreword; Mrs Joyce Bown of Steventon for providing me with many details of unrecorded local history; Mr Philip Carter of Steventon, who knew what a farr milch-cow was; Mr Jeff Dodgson of Steventon for providing his photographs and most kindly giving permission for them to be used in this booklet; Mrs Penelope Hughes-Hallett, Mrs Miranda Tennant, and Mr John Fairbairn, for memories of their childhood at Steventon House; Miss Helen Lefroy for kindly providing a transcript of Anna Lefroy's comments on Steventon in the early nineteenth century, from a manuscript in her possession; Mr Eddie Male for information about the Methodist chapel in Steventon; Mrs Jane Odiwe for drawing the map; and the staff of the Hampshire Record Office for supplying copies of Steventon wills and other documents.

FOREWORD
by the Revd Michael Kenning,
Rector of St. Nicholas, Steventon

Steventon village and its church may not feature prominently in the guide-books and tourist maps of southern England; Hampshire, after all, can boast far grander and more extensive attractions than a small village! Yet, for those who admire and love the writings of Jane Austen, Steventon weaves its own particular charm. The village, almost totally untouched by modern development and no larger in lay-out and population than in Jane's day, enables its visitors to step back in time and to breathe in something of the atmosphere and surroundings which Jane knew. For the greater part of her life – some 25 years – this was Jane's home and the arena within which her talent and skill as a writer originated and matured. It is no exaggeration to claim that many of the images and life-pictures Jane gained from her time in Steventon proved inspirational for passages in her novels – especially so in relation to the three novels composed whilst she lived here.

Through much painstaking research undertaken by Deirdre Le Faye, this book greatly enriches our knowledge and appreciation of Steventon's history. By focussing initially on the early centuries of its history, a picture is gained of the inheritance that was Jane's as a resident of the village. Then through a series of fascinating cameos, drawn from the parish records and the letters of Jane Austen, the essence of village life in Steventon is admirably captured. Yet this book offers more than just an historical survey and a step back in time; it also outlines how the legacy which Jane and her family bequeathed to the village has been developed. A valuable heritage is indeed Steventon's and if future generations are to find delight and enrichment in Jane Austen's life and work that heritage needs to be sustained. Thanks to this book both the village community and all who visit Steventon will be greatly encouraged in that endeavour.

LIST OF ILLUSTRATIONS

The copyright of each photograph used in this publication is acknowledged and attributed to the rightful owners.

Front cover: Elm Tree Cottage at The Triangle
© jd photography

Back cover: the remains of the old rectory pump in the field, with some of
the Bassett's Farm dairy herd
© Deirdre Le Faye

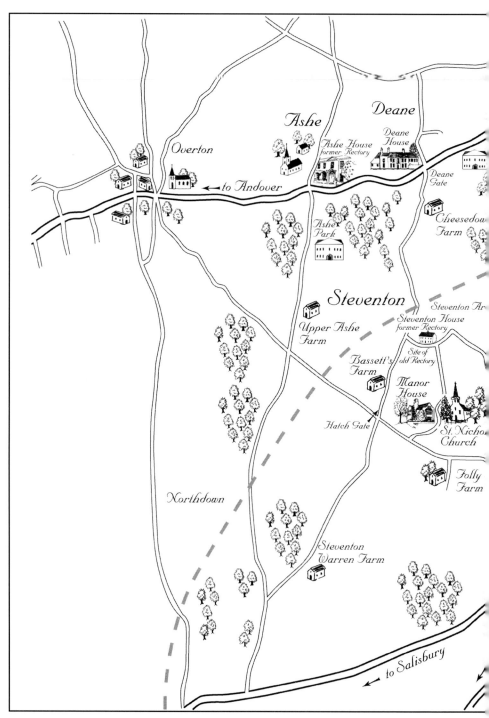

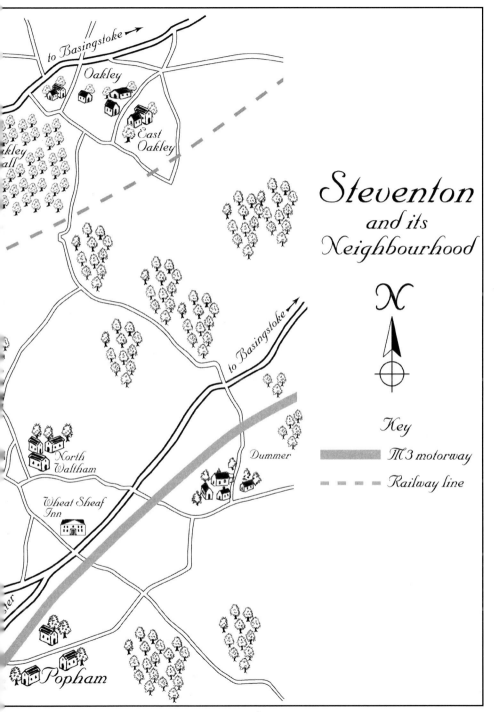

Steventon
and its
Neighbourhood

Key

M3 motorway

Railway line

1. Steventon seen from the west (Burley Lane) – a drawing made in the mid-nineteenth century

JANE AUSTEN'S STEVENTON

The parish and its early days

Steventon is a very peaceful small village tucked away in the north-east corner of Hampshire; its farm-houses and cottages straggle along the lane which leads south from the Deane Gate Inn at the junction with the old stage-coach route to Basingstoke and Andover (now the B3400), down to the even older road that the Romans created to link London with Winchester (now the A30/A33). Halfway along Steventon Lane, the North Waltham lane branches off to the east, and this T-junction, nicknamed 'The Triangle', is the present-day centre of the village, marked by a sign-post, a modern village hall and a bus shelter.

Thomas Carlyle, the Victorian social philosopher, declared: "Happy the people whose annals are blank in history books!" – and this lack of historical record certainly applies to Steventon. It lies hidden from the two main roads, has never been the scene of battles or uprisings, and never had any castle, monastery, or huge mansion to attract travellers down the centuries and provide a focal point for National Trust or English Heritage visitors in recent years. It does, however, possess its own happy and unique claim to fame – that it is the birthplace of Jane Austen, who is now perhaps England's best-known and best-loved novelist.

A friend of Jane Austen's wrote in 1792: "There is something pleasing and pastoral in the scenery hereabouts. Broken ground, green valleys, sheep-clad knolls, and gentle hills covered with wood, and openings through the boles of trees into the neighbouring open country, have a very delightful effect here, especially in spring." The passage of two hundred years has luckily made no great change to this description, though the wandering flocks of sheep have disappeared and been replaced by arable crops and dairy herds. The parish of Steventon is a long narrow strip of land, three miles long by one mile wide, running approximately north/south and lying 450 feet above sea level, and amounting to just over 2000 acres; the subsoil is chalk with flints and includes clay and gravel outcrops, which allows for both heathland, woodland, fields for cultivation and meadows for grazing. The church, St Nicholas, is three-quarters of a mile away from the village, situated on the crest of rising ground 100 feet higher than Steventon Lane, and approached by an even smaller lane called Church Walk. The neighbouring parishes are Ashe, Deane and North Waltham, and the nearest town is Basingstoke, about six miles away.

Steventon's origins probably lie in the Romano-British settlement of Popham, some two miles to the south, where, early in the nineteenth century, the foundations of a large villa were found close to the Wheatsheaf Inn on the main road; in addition another large but plain Romano-British building was discovered in the mid-twentieth century actually in the grounds of Steventon manor house, opposite the church. The villa and its Romanised inhabitants would have traded along the main road with Calleva Atrebatum (the modern Silchester) and with the bigger city of Venta Belgarum (the modern Winchester). When the Roman empire collapsed during the fifth century AD, the Romano-British were left defenceless against the marauding sea-borne immigrants – Jutes, Angles, Saxons – from what is now modern Denmark and Germany, who invaded Hampshire northwards from Southampton Water and southwards from the Thames Valley. Calleva was rapidly deserted, and its foundations now lie under farmland; perhaps some of its residents joined those living at Popham and everyone then fled from the dangerously exposed villa on the main road to become subsistence farmers squatting in agricultural buildings hidden in the woodlands on the rising ground to the north, thus creating the nucleus of the settlement of Steventon.

The Anglo-Saxon invaders won the day, and Steventon acquired its Old English name, though there is a difference of opinion as to its precise meaning. It might come from a personal name – *Stif-ing-tun*, the tun or homestead of Stif's people, or it might be *Sty-ficing-tun*, the homestead at the place of grubbed-up trees. The invaders were pagan, worshipping the Old Norse gods, until the missionary St Birinus came from Rome in the seventh century AD specifically to convert the people of Wessex (south-western England) to Christianity. He was followed in the eighth century by

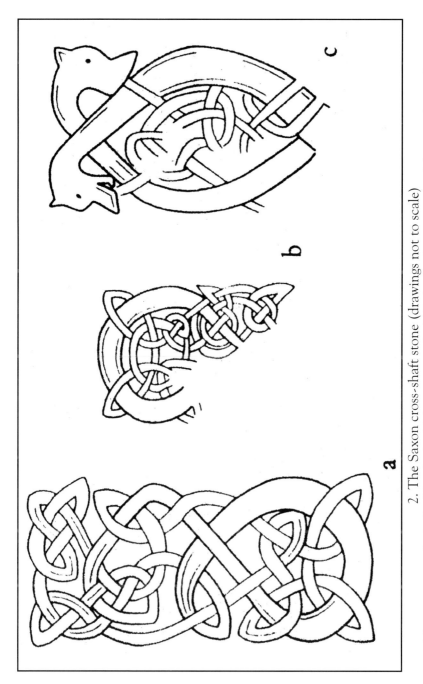

2. The Saxon cross-shaft stone (drawings not to scale)
(a) upper part of side B; (b) side A; (c) lower part of side B; by kind permission of the British Academy

St Boniface of Crediton, who had been a monk first at Exeter and then at Nursling near Southampton; and finally St Swithun, a local man, became Bishop of Winchester in the ninth century, by which time the conversion of Wessex was complete. The first tangible proof of Steventon's existence is the survival of a slab of limestone from the shaft of a preaching-cross, which was probably set up on or near the site of the present church to provide a meeting place where priests from Winchester could deliver sermons to the villagers gathered around. The stone is part of a tapering shaft, now much weathered but showing on one side a panel with two intertwined dragon-like animals, and on the other a pattern of interlacing strap-work, and is probably to be dated to the late eighth or early ninth century. The Steventon stone is similar to a group of sculptures which are widely distributed in Wessex, so perhaps it was St Boniface who encouraged wandering masons to follow him on his missionary journeys around Hampshire and set up crosses wherever possible. The stone was discovered at Steventon Manor House in 1877, and was given to St Nicholas's church in 1952, where it is now on display. A Saxon knife was also discovered in the grounds of the Manor House in 1948, and is now in Basingstoke Museum.

Nothing more is known about the village until Domesday Book was compiled in 1086, which is the first document to give us the names of two of the inhabitants and some indication of the size of the settlement. Although William the Conqueror had ruled England for twenty years since winning the Battle of Hastings in 1066, he had no precise information as to the value of the lands he had seized, and so set his commissioners the task of creating this unique taxation record. They travelled around England, noting the size of the estates, who had owned them in 1066 before the Conquest and who owned them now in 1086, their respective values in 1066 and 1086, and how many people lived in each village. Translated from the Latin and the abbreviated technical jargon of the entries, the information recorded was that in 1066 the main estate at Steventon had amounted to about 600 acres – sufficient to keep five ox-drawn plough teams busy during the year – which was held by the Saxon Alfhelm and valued at 100 shillings. There was also a small estate, of about 60 acres, held by Godwin the Falconer, valued at 4 shillings. Twenty years later, in 1086, the main estate was held by one of William's personal servants, Alfsi the Valet, the land in cultivation was only 360 acres, and its value had dropped from 100 shillings to 70 shillings immediately post-conquest, only now creeping back to 80 shillings. Did Alfhelm and some of his villagers get killed at Hastings in 1066, leaving too few ploughmen to till the fields? Godwin the Falconer had evidently made his peace with the Norman invaders, and been allowed to keep his small estate. Apart from the two lords of the manors, there were five villagers, three smallholders and eight serfs or slaves; assuming that each of these heads of households had a wife and perhaps three children, the total population of Steventon might have been about 90 souls.

After Domesday Book, this first great jumping-off point in the history of modern England, more and more written information about Steventon, its lands and inhabitants, gradually accumulates. The clerks to the royal household – the origins of our modern Civil Service – kept records of land ownership and monies that could be raised by taxation; the bishops of Winchester kept records of the parsons who served the church of St Nicholas; as the population gradually became literate, wills and other personal documents were written, some of which survive in Hampshire Record Office; and finally, from 1841 onwards census returns give us snapshots of the village every decade up to 1901.

The estate, the lords of the manor, and their manor houses

Alfhelm the Saxon and Godwin the Falconer probably lived in hall-houses constructed of timber and thatch, which were the normal building materials of the age. After Domesday, there is no news of Steventon for another century, by which time the two estates had been amalgamated and were in the possession of the Norman family of de Luvers; they built a stone manor-house for themselves, possibly importing the stone from Binstead in the Isle of Wight, as there is no good building stone elsewhere in Hampshire, and this Norman manor-house survived until the sixteenth century. The last of the de Luvers, Geoffrey, died in 1231, leaving Steventon to his two nephews, Hugh de Wengham and Philip de Sandervill, the sons of his sisters. This divided ownership may have suggested to envious neighbours a weakness which could be exploited, and Geoffrey des Roches, a kinsman of the rich, powerful and ruthless Bishop of Winchester, Peter des Roches, moved in for the attack. The Bishop had been the guardian and foster-father of young King Henry III, so it was not surprising that Henry soon declared that the de Luvers family could not make good their claim to hold Steventon, and instead bestowed it upon Geoffrey des Roches in 1233. Hugh and Philip fought off Geoffrey for a time, by paying £80 (an enormous sum in those days) to the king in 1234 to recover their estate; but by 1250 Geoffrey's son Martin had bought the de Sandervill share, and completed his takeover by buying the de Wengham share in 1260.

The des Roches family lived at Steventon for the next century, holding the estate by the serjeanty [service or obligation] of providing one man-at-arms on horseback to serve in the King's army for forty days, whenever called upon to do so. This particular serjeanty may perhaps account for the unusual names of Upper and Lower Quintons being given to two fields close to the manor house, suggesting that this was where the would-be soldiers underwent their military training. To manage a horse with one hand, hold a long lance with the other, charge at an enemy and succeed in knocking him off his horse without losing one's own balance, required much practice, and a *quintain* was part of the training equipment. It was a tall post, with a loaded top or cross-piece, which provided a target for the charge. If the quintain was hit fair and square, the rider could gallop quickly by unscathed, but if hit off-target, the loaded cross-piece would swing round and thump the rider on the back with a sandbag or wooden plank.

In 1361 the des Roches family died out in the male line, and Steventon, as well as other estates, became the property of Mary, their last heiress. She now married Sir Bernard Brocas, who lived at Beaurepaire in the nearby parish of Sherborne St John, and who was the most notable lord of the manor that Steventon ever possessed. Sir Bernard was a gallant soldier, loyal courtier and efficient administrator; the lifelong friend and companion-in-arms of Edward the Black Prince, he probably fought alongside him at Crécy and Poitiers, and was at various times Constable of Aquitaine and Captain of Calais in France, in England Constable of Corfe Castle and later of Odiham Castle, Captain of Sandgate Castle, Warden of Episcopal Parks,

Master of the Royal Buckhounds, and Chamberlain to King Richard II's wife Queen Anne. In Hampshire he was a Commissioner for Defence and a Knight of the Shire, sitting in Parliament eight times between 1369 and his death in 1395. He was buried in the Chapel of St Edmund in Westminster Abbey, close to monuments of various members of the royal family whom he had served. The tomb bears a wooden effigy of him, recumbent and dressed in armour; upon his helmet is the Brocas family crest, a Moor's head with an oriental crown, and his shield shows a golden lion rampant on a black background. Perhaps some Steventon men joined Sir Bernard as foot-soldiers in his military commands, but it is quite possible that he never in fact visited this small estate, leaving the management of it to a steward or bailiff from Beaurepaire.

Sir Bernard's son, Sir Bernard II, looked likely to have a similarly successful career, since at the time of his father's death he was already one of King Richard II's courtiers. However, the King was deposed by his cousin Henry Bolingbroke, Duke of Lancaster, in 1399; Richard's supporters, of whom the loyal Sir Bernard was one, attempted to reinstate him early in 1400; but their uprising was defeated and, as Bolingbroke by now had been crowned King Henry IV, such an uprising was classed as treason. Sir Bernard was tried and condemned at the Tower of London on 4th February 1400, and the following day walked to Tyburn gallows for his execution, his headless body being buried in the church of the London Greyfriars. Henry IV was not vindictive towards the Brocas family, and Bernard's widow and children were allowed to keep their estates; understandably, for several generations to come the family preferred to live unobtrusively as Hampshire landowners rather than dangerously as courtiers.

By the end of the fifteenth century, the Brocas family came to an end with an heiress, Edith, who married Ralph Pexall, a royal clerk (that is, a senior civil servant); they both died about 1520 and are buried in St Andrew's church in Sherborne St John, with lifesize effigies on their tomb. Their son Sir Richard Pexall succeeded to the Brocas estate at Beaurepaire, and returned to the family tradition of attendance at court, becoming a loyal supporter of Queen Mary Tudor, who commended him for his 'good, true and faithful service'. He decided to build a new manor house for himself at Steventon, so in 1560 demolished the old Norman house and

3. The Brocas manor house, as it was in the late nineteenth century

re-used its stones, together with the local flints, in the construction of what was intended to be just one wing of a large mansion. As near as can now be estimated, the wing was about 120 feet long by 20 feet wide; it had cellars and three storeys above, with a shallow porch on the east side running up the height of the house, huge chimney-stacks, mullioned windows, and a large bay window at the north end. But Sir Richard died in 1571, and lack of funds in succeeding generations meant that no more than this one wing of the new house was ever built. Like his ancestor Sir Bernard Brocas, Sir Richard Pexall is commemorated in St Edmund's chapel in Westminster Abbey by a large wall-monument, where he and his two wives are shown as kneeling profile figures in niches surrounded by columns.

Sir Richard's widow, Dame Elinor, lived on at Beaurepaire and married again, and in true fairy-tale style she and her new husband Sir John Savage did their best to usurp the lands and rights of their step-daughter, the heiress Anne Pexall. Anne married a distant cousin, another Bernard Brocas, but the young couple were never able to occupy Beaurepaire while the Savages were in possession. Their son, Sir Pexall Brocas, born in 1563, was based at Steventon but wasted his fortunes in London; in 1603 he was charged with riot, and with forging and publishing a forged deed of perjury, and he was popularly credited with begetting an enormous number of illegitimate children. According to the London historian John Stow: 'On Sunday, October 24, 1613, Sir Pecsall Brocas did open penance at Paul's Cross [a public meeting place outside Old St Paul's Cathedral]; he stood in a white sheete, and held a stick in his hand, having been formerly convicted before the High Commissioners for secret and notorious adulteries with divers women.' Not in the least abashed, Sir Pexall then went with 'thirty men in scarlet that waited upon him, to the Lord Mayor, to demand a dinner after doing penance'.

Steventon manor passed to Sir Pexall's only legitimate son and heir, Thomas Brocas, who lived there for a time in the early seventeenth century – the baptisms of three of his children, Elizabeth (1610), Prudence (1617), and Thomas (1619), are recorded in the parish registers – before he was eventually able to reclaim Beaurepaire in 1626. Thanks to his father's extravagances, Thomas was deep in debt, so during the next twenty years he leased out and mortgaged Steventon before finally selling the estate to the sitting tenants, the Mynne family, in 1648, thus ending the Brocas ownership after nearly 300 years.

During the seventeenth century it became more and more difficult to keep the ownership of Steventon within the line of family descent, as sons died young or unmarried and daughters' marriages proved sterile. The Mynne heir, George, died in 1651, and the estate passed to his sister Anne, the wife of Sir John Lewkenor of West Dean in Sussex. The Lewkenors' son John died childless in 1706, and he could find no-one nearer in blood to whom to bequeath Steventon than a second cousin, William Woodward. William was married to another Lewkenor cousin, Elizabeth Martin; but as Elizabeth was in her own right heiress to the estate of the Knight family at Chawton, a Hampshire village some fifteen miles away from Steventon, he was obliged to change his name to Knight in order to share in his wife's property. William Woodward Knight died in 1721 and Elizabeth married again in 1725 Bulstrode Peachey, who likewise had to change his name to Knight. Both marriages were childless, so Madam Knight – as she was known – had to look even further back on the family tree for an heir to her Hampshire estates. She chose a distant cousin, on the maternal side, of her first husband William Woodward – Thomas Brodnax of Godmersham in Kent. Thomas Brodnax had already changed his name to May in order to inherit property from that family, and changed it yet again to Knight in 1738, when he succeeded Madam Knight in the ownership of both Steventon and Chawton.

In 1741 Mr Knight commissioned maps of his newly-acquired Hampshire properties, and from these it can be seen that Steventon Manor Farm, at 1350 acres, covered nearly all the parish; there was also New Farm of 400 acres on the west side of Steventon Lane and including some fields in the parish of Ashe; and the much smaller Street Farm, two separate parcels of land in the north of the parish, of only 200 acres. Mr Knight's estate steward Edward Randall, who lived in Chawton, wrote detailed letters to his employer about the problems he found to exist at Steventon: in 1743 Parker, the outgoing tenant of the Manor Farm, had let the barns fall into disrepair, and Hellear, the incoming tenant, did not know where to start rebuilding, "for now the Barns are empty the defects do appear to be so bad as no one could be sensible of before." However, Hellear in his turn proved a bad tenant, and Mr Knight commented to Randall: "I find Mr. Hellear acts upon the same Principles with other Hampshire Farmers, that a Tenant on leaving a Farm has a right to rob it of all he can, & leave it for the Landlord to make good the Damage to the next Tenant." At the end of 1757 Mr Knight wrote: "I am glad a Person of Credit & Circumstances has enquired after Steventon Farm ... & as to his saying the Rent is too dear, when at the same time he says, he knows it only in part, and has not look'd over it, is only declaring that whatever the value of a Farm is, the Rent must be abated; which is at present the unreasonable Argument of the Hampshire Farmers. However, when you hear from this Mr. Digweed you'll let me know his Proposals." The brothers Hugh and Richard Digweed took possession in the summer of 1758; their initial tenancy was for 15 years, but in fact they and their descendants stayed on until 1877, and several members of the family are later mentioned in Jane Austen's letters.

The Digweeds' first improvements were the digging of a new pond 20 yards square at Bassett's Buildings (Bassett was a sub-tenant, whose name has endured down the years) in Steventon Lane, at a cost of £40, and repairing the pond on the Warren land for £22. An insurance policy of 1794 shows that the Manor Farm out-buildings then consisted of two stables adjoining, brick-built and tiled roof, a dog kennel of one floor and six bays, a long barn of two floors and ten bays, an oat barn of two floors and twelve bays, and a granary – all these being timber-built and thatched. At Bassett's Buildings there was a wheat barn of one floor and three bays, a barley barn of two floors and eight bays, cart-house and fodder-house adjoining – all likewise timber-built and thatched. A few years later the family erected a large threshing-mill, at a cost of £250, which required four horses, two men and four boys to work it, but which nevertheless was cheaper and quicker than hand-threshing. Perhaps the Digweeds over-reached themselves with this expenditure, because about 1810 they relinquished the southern part of Manor Farm, which was then let separately under the name of Warren Farm.

Although Thomas Brodnax May Knight had several children, only one son, Thomas Knight II, survived to adulthood; and when it became obvious that his marriage to Catherine Knatchbull was going to be childless, he adopted for his heir yet another distant cousin, young Edward Austen, the third son of the Revd George Austen, rector of Steventon. Edward spent much time with his adoptive parents at Godmersham and inherited all three estates when Thomas Knight II died in 1794, finally changing his name to Knight when the widowed Mrs Catherine Knight died in 1812. It is thanks to the archives of the Knight and Austen families that so much is known about Steventon during the eighteenth and nineteenth centuries.

Edward Austen Knight died at Godmersham in 1852, and by then his eldest son, Edward Knight II, was thoroughly settled at Chawton Great House, had married twice and had a correspondingly large family to support. He therefore put Steventon on the market in 1854: the New Farm was now being referred to as Bassett's Farm after its earlier tenant, Warren Farm was 490 acres, the northern part of Street Farm had been re-named Cheesedown, and the southern part was now divided into ten small-holdings totalling 144 acres; the total rental was about £12,000 p.a. The following year the estate was bought by the 2nd Duke of Wellington, thus finally ending any Lewkenor or Knight family connection with the ownership of Steventon. The Digweeds stayed on as tenants of the Manor Farm; in the early 1860s some of their farm buildings were burnt down by a disgruntled employee named Russell, and the ruins were still visible a century later, lying off a lane going southwards from the church. One of the Digweed grand-daughters married the Revd J. G. Gibbs, and many years later he wrote: "My first visit to Steventon was after our marriage, in 1864 or 5. This was after the ancient farm buildings had been destroyed by fire but I remember the well-house, which escaped, with its great wheel worked by a donkey – like Carisbrooke [Castle, on the Isle of Wight] – Also the great drawing room over 40 feet long & the dining room, not much less."

The Duke sold the estate in 1877, to a wealthy retired corn-factor, Mr Henry Harris, and the last Digweed – John-James, an elderly bachelor – moved out. Mr Harris started off by planning to refurbish and enlarge the old Brocas manor house, but lost enthusiasm for this idea when a skeleton was discovered under the dining-room floor. Instead, he chose a new site within the manor house grounds, and during the next five years erected there a mansion in bright red brick, said to have been designed by the architect Waterhouse ' in the Tudor style'. It had pointed turrets, gables, tall

4. The Harris manor house, about 1900

chimney-stacks and mullioned windows, and looked like a small version of the Midland Grand Hotel at St Pancras railway station in London. There was 'extensive cellarage' underneath the whole house; on the ground floor there were two oak-panelled halls, large dining- and drawing-rooms, library, billiard-room and study, plus all the necessary working quarters for the servants, and upstairs were 22 bed- and dressing-rooms, three bathrooms, a school room, and housemaids' rooms. The house had its own electricity generator, which provided lighting and also pumped water from the 160-ft deep well up into storage tanks in the roof. A separate stable block could accommodate seven horses along with carriages and grooms' quarters. The Brocas manor house was stripped out and converted into stables for another dozen horses, with workshop, saddle- and harness-rooms. This was presumably the occasion when the Saxon cross-shaft stone came to light, as Harris recorded that it had been 'found built into the walls of the old Manor House' – and it was later rebuilt into the wall of the front porch of the new house.

Mr Harris rebuilt the central block of Bassett's Farm, and also built a new separate house to the south of it – this was at one time called Home Farm, but in 1990 was re-named Oakdown House. The original Bassett's Farmhouse is the building standing at the entrance to the farmyard, which for some years now has been divided into two cottages. Mr Harris also added several new cottages to the village's housing stock, and in 1893 he built Steventon's first proper school, with room for 60 pupils, and a house for two teachers adjoining, at a cost of £1,200. He improved the gradient of Church Walk – some small cuttings can still be seen, buttressed by walls of flint and brick, while in other places the lane is embanked slightly above the level of the surrounding fields – and provided neat iron railings to demarcate the roadway from the fields.

Mr Harris died in 1898 and his son, Henry Harris junior, sold the Manor House in 1910 to Mr and Mrs Robert Mills. Mr Mills died in 1921, and his widow sold out in 1928 to Mr and Mrs Jack Onslow Fane. During the 1920s-30s the estate flourished, and was well-known in agricultural circles for its pedigree stock of Shorthorn cattle, Hampshire Down sheep, Large White pigs, Shire horses and racehorses. Its woodlands provided excellent shooting – pheasants, partridges, hares and rabbits, these last no doubt

5. The Fane manor house, about 1935

chiefly on Warren Farm. Also at this period two private railway sidings were laid out, joined on to the main London-Southampton line where it passed through Northdown Plantation, with the key to their gates being kept at the signal box nearby. These sidings may perhaps have been used to bring in supplies of coal and building materials to the Manor House, or possibly cattle trucks were attached to trains when livestock had to be moved.

In 1932 the Harris manor house was destroyed by fire – luckily with no loss of life – and only the separate stable block and the remains of the Brocas house survived. The Onslow Fanes returned to the Brocas house, refurbished it, and added two more wings of flint and stone, which were far more in keeping with the original design than the Victorian red-brick version had been. However, after going to all this trouble, they left in 1936, selling the new house to Captain Bernard Hutton Croft, who enjoyed the good shooting on the well-wooded estate. Following the outbreak of war, in 1940 the house was commandeered by the London Fire Service as a training centre and home for a bomb disposal squad, and the Hutton Crofts were displaced to live nearby in the rectory (now called Steventon House). They never moved back into the Manor House; for a time in 1947-48 part of it was used as a private school called Hilsea College, but thereafter it remained unoccupied. Captain Hutton Croft died in 1961 and his wife in 1967; the Hutton Croft cousin to whom it was bequeathed sold it in 1969 to the Mackinnon family, who likewise lived in Steventon House as the Manor House was by now vandalised and derelict. It was finally demolished in 1970, with its rubble being used in the construction of the M3 motorway to the south of the parish.

The only surviving remnant of the Manor House complex was the Victorian stable-block, which in the 1970s was used variously as a barn and machinery store, and to house a grass-seed drying plant. In 1975 it was swept out and cleaned and used as a hall for the play-readings which formed part of the celebrations for the bicentenary of Jane Austen's birth. This block was sold in 1986 as 'Steventon Manor Stables', and converted into a sizeable family home, with a separate unit of garage and staff accommodation built alongside. This house is now known as Steventon Manor, and has already had several changes of ownership in the past twenty years.

6. The present manor house, about 2000   © jd photography

7. St. Nicholas's church, southern side   © jd photography

Bassetts Farm and Warren Farm were sold off as freehold properties in the 1980s, and Stoken Farm now occupies 600 acres in the north of the parish. The modern crops are mainly wheat and oilseed rape, with some barley, oats, sainfoin, and occasionally turnips. Maize and grass are grown to make winter silage feed for dairy herds.

The church, its rectors and rectory

The church is dedicated to St Nicholas, a legendary figure said to have been the Bishop of Myra in Turkey in the fourth century AD, whose cult was very popular in the eastern Mediterranean region for several centuries. He is reputed to have given bags of gold to three young girls for their marriage dowries in order to save them from a life of prostitution, and another tale is that he brought back to life three little boys who had been murdered; because of this patronage of children, the custom later developed in Europe of giving them presents on his feast day, 6th December, and in this connection his name became corrupted into Santa Claus. The saint's relics were moved to Bari in southern Italy in 1087, where the English soldiers stopped off on their journeys to and from the Holy Land during the First Crusade of 1096-99, hence his cult was brought to England at this time and in due course over 400 churches were dedicated to him.

Steventon church was built by the then lords of the manor, the de Luvers family, probably about the year 1200. It has changed very little over the centuries, and consists simply of a nave 44 feet by 20 feet, and a chancel 20 feet by 15 feet 6 inches, with a small enclosed bell-turret or tower at the west end, above the west door. Three small bells hang in the tower, two medieval and the third dated 1670. The church's walls are of the local flint, rendered over, with Binstead stone for the window and door frames. In the thirteenth century the chancel was partly rebuilt and the main doorway moved from the south wall of the nave to its present position at the base of the tower, facing west, replacing an existing lancet window; the original door was probably where the west window on the south wall is now. The east wall and window were rebuilt in the fifteenth century, and in 1533 a wealthy parishioner left a bequest to pay for the church's reroofing with one thousand wooden shingles. At this pre-Reformation date other parishioners left bequests to pay for lights before the various images (presumably wooden figures rather than paintings) of Jesus, Our Lady of Comfort, St Nicholas and St Anthony, and there was also another altar to the Virgin Mary on the north side of the church.

During the seventeenth century a large box-pew, made of thin oak boards, was erected at the eastern end of the nave, opposite the pulpit, for the benefit of the lords of the manor; at some time in the early part of the twentieth century it was moved to the western end of the nave, where it now serves as a vestry. On its wall hang two Rolls of Honour, with the names of the 66 inhabitants of Steventon who served in the two World Wars, including the five who died on active service – Richard Barrett, James Beale, James Hedges, Barry Isles and Leslie Roe. The present spire was erected about 1850-60, a belated replacement of one that had blown down in the previous century. Also in the nineteenth century stained glass windows, pews, pulpit and choir stalls were added, and the font – which presumably was the original one dating to the foundation of the church – was replaced in 1868 by one of white marble, given by the Digweed family. The altar and the stained glass window above it date from the 1880s, and both were placed in the church as a memorial to the Revd John-James Digweed, the last of the family to tenant the Manor House. His cousin, William-Henry Digweed, at his death in 1881 bequeathed £100 to be used for the benefit of the parish, and the investment income of £2.9s.4d. p.a. was for some years used to pay for a distribution of coal. In 1912 the Mills family gave a small organ, which is placed on the north side of the chancel. In 1952 Captain and Mrs Hutton Croft presented the stone from the Saxon cross-shaft, and this is on display inside the church. The present side altar was brought in from Litchfield Methodist Chapel by the Revd Basil Norris and consecrated in Steventon in 1971. During renovations in 1988, a double piscina and niche were uncovered in the south wall, and a fireplace was found in the north wall. In the latter part of the twentieth century, repairs and renovations have been ongoing, with the generous assistance of the English Jane Austen Society and the Jane Austen Society of North America (JASNA), including the provision of a new font cover as a millenium gift in 2000.

THE SQUIRE'S PEW

8. The box pew – drawing by Ellen Hill, 1900

21

The church plate consists of a silver chalice and paten cover of 1663, a paten of 1722, and a flagon of 1867, this last given by the Digweed family in that year. A pair of hand-carved oak candlesticks for the altar is the most recent addition, dedicated in 2006 in memory of the late Joseph Bown of Bassetts Farm, who was for many years one of the churchwardens. The church also possesses a handsomely-bound large Bible, printed in 1793, and given to St Nicholas by the Revd George Austen, which is occasionally used for special services.

The church contains several contemporary memorials to members of Jane Austen's family: her grandmother Mrs Jane Leigh, her eldest brother James and his two wives, Anne Mathew and Mary Lloyd, her nephew William Knight and three little daughters of his who died in a scarlet fever epidemic in 1848; there is also a modern plaque commemorating Jane herself, placed in the nave in 1936 by her great-grand-niece Miss Emma Austen-Leigh. There are a number of other gravestones and memorials to members of the Digweed family.

Outside the church stands a broad-crowned hollow yew tree which, when measured in 1998, had a girth of 25 feet. It is popularly believed that yews can live for millennia, but this is very unlikely, and churchyard yews are probably no older than the site of the church itself, which would mean that the Steventon yew is about 800 years old.

As there is no bedrock in the parish, there are only a few early gravestones in the churchyard, because the raw material for such memorials would have been difficult and expensive to transport. It was probably only the coming of the railway in the 1840s which enabled the residents to bring in, for example, granite slabs or cast-iron crosses, and most of the headstones and ledger-stones now in existence are of the nineteenth and twentieth centuries. The earliest surviving stone which is still legible is that of John Cooper, who died 22nd September 1767 aged 23; he lies next to his married sister Elizabeth Waterman who died in 1779. Jane Austen's brother James shares a vault with his second wife Mary, and next to this is the vault of her nephew the Revd William Knight and his three wives, together with four of his children who died in infancy. Several members of the Digweed family are buried here, as well as having memorial tablets inside the church, and other owners of the Manor House also chose to remain close to their old home – Henry Harris and his wife Janet, the Mills family, Jack Onslow Fane and Captain and Mrs Hutton Croft.

As the de Luvers family had built the church, they had therefore the advowson or patronage of it – that is, the right to present a cleric of their choice to the bishop of Winchester, who would then officially instal the candidate as rector of St Nicholas. In 1238 the de Luvers heirs Hugh de Wengham and Philip de Sandervill formally agreed that they and their families would take it in turns to present a rector, but their candidates are not recorded. A list of all the known rectors as appearing in the Winchester registers is given on page 56, but many of them are no more than names echoing faintly down the centuries. The first of whom any personal record survives is Geoffrey de Monteney, who in 1301 was granted three years' study-leave from Steventon; but like all too many students, he ran into debt, and in 1305 was in court at Westminster being ordered to pay back £7.7s.2d. to Richard de Middeltone. When the Black Death – now considered to have been bubonic plague – arrived in Hampshire in 1349, the priests tending the dying themselves caught the infection and died equally rapidly. At Steventon the only young man available for installation in 1349 was Geoffrey (or Walter) de Brokhampton, who was no more than an acolyte – the most minor of all the clerical orders – and the bishop's register shows that he was rushed through the grades of sub-deacon, deacon, and finally priest, in a matter of four weeks, a progression which would normally have taken several years. How long Geoffrey survived is not known – the chaos and panic of the plague-time meant that no proper records were kept.

These early rectors probably lived close to the church and manor-house in some cottage of which no trace remains; but it would seem that from at least the sixteenth century the rectory was sited at the corner of Church Walk and the North Waltham lane, in a shallow valley surrounded by sloping meadows dotted with elm trees, and with about half a dozen cottages close by on each side of the lane. This parsonage house survived until the 1820s, and in 1775 was the birthplace of Jane Austen.

In 1543, when John Bennett was rector, Bishop Gardiner made a formal visitation to the village, and left instructions that the churchyard walls should be repaired. There is now no trace of any walls, so presumably these were only made of cob or chalk. In the next century a record was created

– the Revd John Orpwood was installed as rector in 1602, and stayed until his death in 1658 – a tenure of 56 years, which has never been surpassed. Mr Orpwood's son, John junior, was also in Holy Orders and took over the parish in 1661, but did not survive as long and healthily as his father had done; in 1694 the churchwardens and inhabitants of Steventon petitioned the Bishop of Winchester to take the revenues of the church into his own hands and use them to pay the salary of a curate, Benjamin Wells, because Mr Orpwood was in his 'second childhood' – or as we would now diagnose, suffering from Alzheimer's disease.

The Revd Richard Deane, from Climping in Sussex, was presented by the Lewkenor family in 1695; judging from his will he seems to have been a rather pedantic, anxious man, and upon arrival at Steventon made a careful list, with the assistance of his two churchwardens, of exactly what he could expect to occupy and earn in his new position. This list, known officially as a glebe terrier, gives a snapshot of the rectory at the end of the seventeenth century:

"Imprimis the Church-yard, fenced all round by the parishioners, viz: the East, South, and West sides by the Lord of the Manor, and the North side by the other Inhabitants, whose particular Shares are proportionably alloted according to the value of theire respective Livings. Except the Gate, which is maintained by the Rector.

"The Parsonage-house, consisting of two Bays of building, & outletted at the west end, and part of the south side over the Celler.

"One barn, with a porch, consisting of three Bays of building, outletteded [sic] all round.

"One lesser barn, consisting of three Bays of building, with a stable at the East end thereof.

"One close of gleib-land adjoining to the said parsonage house and barns, which (together with the Gateroom garden and orchard) is by estimaton two acres & an half.

"One parcell of gleib-land lying in the midle-common-field, adjoining to the hedge of the said field on the East, and to a pitt (formerly a chalk-dell) on the west, having the Lands of the Widdow Passion now in the possession of Joseph Cocks, on the south; and the Lands of Mr Richard

Woodruff now in the possession of Thomas Webb on the North, and is by estimaton half an acre.

"There hath formerly been (by common Fame) a great deal more gleib-land belonging to the said Rectory, which lyeth dispersedly among the lands of the Lord of the Mannor, and hath been detain from the Church beyond the memory of man; of which Wee can give no other account than by tradition.

"The Rector of Steventon hath ever had, & still hath all maner of tythes, both great & small, of what nature & quality soever, arising within the said parish, except from certaine lands, lying at Litchfield, within the said parish, comonly called Tythe-free.

"The Rector of Steventon hath ever had, & still hath from every house within the said parish five eggs, payable yearly on Good fryday.

"The Rector of Steventon hath, for a Cowe-wite, two pence, and for a farr-milch Cowe, three halfpence.

"For a marryage (the banns being thrice asked) one Shilling & Sixpence.

"And for Churching a woman, sixpence."

The reference to cows arises from the fact that the herbage of the churchyard was itself part of the rector's property, and only he was entitled to graze his livestock upon it; hence if someone else's cow broke in and was caught grazing, the owner would have to pay the rector a fine of two pence. A reduction of a halfpenny was made if the beast in question was a 'farr' milch cow – that is, a favourite or pet house-cow kept for one family's benefit alone.

Ironically, Mr Deane had little time left to worry about his house and income, for he died early in 1697. The inventory of his personal goods and chattels shows a total value of £59: £5 in money and clothes, £8-worth of books, some very sparse furnishings in the five rooms of the rectory (only two up and two down, with a kitchen tacked on at the side) totalling £10.10s., £5-worth of brass and pewter utensils, livestock (four cows, one horse, five hogs and ten pigs) totalling £20, and £10-worth of corn stored in the barn with another 10 shillings'-worth still in the ground.

His successor was Thomas Church, a young man with a wife and in due course ten children, five of whom were baptised in Steventon. They must have found it very difficult to fit into so small a rectory, but perhaps Mr Church was rich enough to build on another room or two, for he was able to leave his children quite substantial sums of money when he died in 1720; he must also have been devoted to the parish he had served, as he gave instructions in his will that he was to be buried in the chancel of St Nicholas.

During the eighteenth century much more information about the church, rectory and rectors becomes available, as the bishops of Winchester and the Knight family both take a closer interest in the parish and record their findings in registers and correspondence. In 1725 the Bishop sent out a questionnaire to all the parsons in his diocese, and the Revd Richard Wright, Thomas Church's successor since 1721, replied: there were about 80 souls in the parish, and the yearly average was one or two marriages, one or two burials, and three or four births. The patroness was Madam Knight of Chawton; there was no chapel, no lecturer or curate, no Papists, no Dissenters; no resident nobility or gentry; no school, charity or hospital.

Mr Wright did not live long, and in 1727 John Church, the second son of the Revd Thomas, came back to his former home. He and his churchwardens compiled "A Terryer of ye Lands belonging to ye Rectory of Steventon: 1 Acre & an half adjoining to ye Parsonage House; ½ an Acre in ye middle-Common Field on ye upper-side, one end whereof runs up to ye hither Field Hedge pointing towards ye East the other terminates about half a rod." They also wrote out "A schedule of the Goods belonging to the Parish Church of Steventon. Imprimis: To the Alter [sic] 1 Table, 1 Green & 1 White Cloth, 1 Pewter Flaggon, 1 Sylver Chalice, 1 small Sylver Pattin. Item To the Body of ye Church 1 Green Pulpit Cushion, 1 Surplice, 1 Bible, 1 Common Prayer Book, 1 Font, 1 Bier, 1 Ladder, 3 Bells, 1 Chest." The cushion was used to support the large and heavy Bible as the rector balanced it on the pulpit edge in front of him during his sermon; the ladder was to reach the bells in the little tower; and the chest would be lockable and contain the church plate when not in use, together with anything else considered of value.

At this period Steventon seems to have been somewhat of an unhealthy place, for several rectors died in quick succession – Richard Wright in

1726, John Church in 1733, David Strahan in 1737, and Henry Haddon in 1743. It was left to the churchwardens to tell the Bishop in August 1733 that the "Church excepting ye Tower in good repair, & yt to be repaird as soon as Harvest is over. Our Minister lately deceased; parsonage house & out housing in good repair. Church-Yard, well fenced." Five years later they reported: "Church &c in good repair. Our Tower is in repairing. Parishioners &c all is well."

Once Mr Knight of Godmersham became lord of the manor, his steward Edward Randall wrote frequently with news of the parish, and in May 1743 dispassionately told of the imminent death of the rector: "Last Tuesday I was at Steventon, I saw Mr. Haddon and's Family ... I believe Mr. Haddon to be past recovery and that he cannot hold it long – tho they say he is better than he has been, I find Dr. Combs has given him his least prescription, vizt to go to Bath, but he says he shall never see it. The Tenants there desire their Duty to you and as in all probability the liveing will very soon fall into your hands to dispose off, they humbly hope that you'll take care (so far as you can) to let them have a good Man, and one who will not be Extortionate about his Tithes" – and a week later: "Mr. Haddon is Dead, & buried last Night ..." It was the responsibility of the tenant of the Manor House to liaise with the rector to keep the church in good repair, but Mr Haddon had neglected to keep any proper records, and although the outgoing tenant Parker claimed to have spent £62.2s.3½d. in this respect, Randall suspected that this sum had been spread over the forty years of Parker's tenancy, "for the Church is Now very much out of repair."

In 1754 the reign, as it might be called, of the Austen family of clergymen commenced at Steventon. The Revd Thomas Bathurst, a maternal cousin of Mr Knight of Godmersham on the Austen side, was presented by him as curate, a position he held until becoming rector of Welwyn, Herts, in 1765. Another cousin, the Revd Henry Austen, was presented by Mr Knight as rector in 1759, but he resigned in 1761 in favour of the better living of West Wickham in Kent. Mr Knight's next choice to benefit from his patronage was a younger cousin, the Revd George Austen, who was currently a don at St John's College in Oxford. George Austen was in no hurry to move to Steventon, perhaps because he was still single and thought it better to get married before leaving Oxford, and so was content to leave the parish in the care of his cousin Thomas Bathurst.

George Austen found himself a wife in the person of Cassandra Leigh, the niece of the Master of Balliol, and the young couple were married in April 1764 and travelled straightaway to Hampshire after the wedding ceremony. They had to live in the rectory at Deane for the first few years, because Steventon rectory was so decrepit; under its red tiled roof the walls were a patchwork of brick, timber framing with brick infills, and weather-tiled lath and plaster. The Revd George Austen and his family lived here until 1801, and during these years he nearly re-built the rectory – eventually it had five rooms on the ground floor, seven bedrooms and three attics. In size and appearance it was probably very much like the cottage in Chawton where Mrs Austen lived in her widowhood with her two daughters, and which has now become the Jane Austen House Museum.

As well as having to rebuild his future home, George Austen arrived in the parish just in time to find the church badly in need of repair. Edward Randall wrote to Mr Knight in February 1764: "The high Winds (which we have had a great deal of this Winter which hath done some damage here and in many places) has blown down Steventon Church Steple, and it has fallen on the roof of the Church and done some damage to that. The Steple was Timber work and Boarded, both sides and Roof, It is a Square Tower of about 11 feet, and comes out of the sides of the Roof, and is carry'd up from thence about 10 feet, to a little above the Ridge, and then a Pyramidall Roof put on it. I was not in the Church to see the foundation, but suppose there must be Timber Work from the Ground to support it, or large Timbers cross the Church from Wall to Wall to support the Tower. The Timbers which are in view are very much decay'd."

A month later Randall wrote another gloomy letter to his employer: "Tuesday I was at Steventon & found Digweed bad with the Rheumatism. He says in a little time You shall have the last Ladydays Rent. I have Examined their Church book for the last 20 Years (but Digweed has kept no Acct. nor enter'd anything in it dureing his time, which I told him I thought very wrong), I find laid out for Repairs of the Church in 1744, £8; in 1755, 17 shillings; in 1756, 17 shillings and five pence; in 1757, 18 shillings; and by Digweed since as he says to this day 1764, £2 and 17 shillings; In all laid

STEVENTON PARSONAGE

9. The old rectory – a wood engraving as used in the *Memoir of Jane Austen*, 1870

out by the Parish in the last 20 Years £13.9s.5d., Chiefly in repairing the Tileing & the Floor. You repaird the Porch &c when Hellear took it. The Belfrey stands on good Arches, but the Timbers above, ie from the foot of the Roof are quite decay'd."

Mr Austen evidently did not attempt to replace the spire but concentrated on patching up the roof, so that in the following year he was able to assure the Bishop of Winchester that "the church and chancel are in good repair, and everything necessary for the celebration of divine service, and the administration of the holy sacrament are provided." It took him four years to make the Steventon rectory habitable for his wife and children (while they were living at Deane the Austens had three sons born), but in the summer of 1768 the family was able to move in; and in due course another five children were born to them here, including Jane in 1775. Although the house itself could be re-built, being sited in a valley meant it was always liable to be damp; and in 1795, when a long snowy winter was followed by a sudden thaw in March, the cellars and ground floor were flooded and the Austens were trapped upstairs for two days.

When Mr Austen decided to retire and moved to Bath in 1801, his eldest son James occupied the Steventon rectory and acted as his father's curate, until himself becoming rector following his father's death in 1805. James had three children – Anna, James-Edward, and Caroline – and their memories, recorded many years later, confirm that the rectory was now an unpretentious but comfortable family home, with a carriage drive linking it to the North Waltham lane, and at the back, on the south side, a large garden producing vegetables and flowers, which was protected from the east wind by a thatched mud wall typical of that part of Hampshire, and overshadowed by fine elm trees. In front of the house, James and his son together planted a lime tree in 1813, as 'a record of our mutual love' and as a tangible reminder for James-Edward in his future life; the tree is still there, and when it was surveyed in May 2000 it had reached a height of 125 ft.

James Austen had been ailing for some years, and the decline in his health became very noticeable during 1818. To the end of her own life, his daughter Caroline remembered with gratitude the devotion shown by the Austens' groom/manservant William Alexander: "He was a very young

10. The lime tree planted by James Austen   *© Deirdre Le Faye*

11. The Knight rectory, built in the 1820s © Deirdre Le Faye

man, but he had been with us two or three years, and he had attached himself so strongly to his master, that all he did for him seemed a labour of love. Up to the last, William assiduously attended on him with a patience and affection that knew no weariness." James died in December 1819, and the grief of his family was aggravated by a flood in January 1820, as Caroline recorded: "A deluge seemed to come to drive us away. It was an unusually severe winter, and much snow fell. A thaw came on suddenly and one night we were roused by the rush of water pouring into the cellars, with the noise of a cataract, and on going down the men found all the ground floor under water. There were drains made on purpose to meet such occurrences, but nobody had thought about them, and so high was the water round the house, that the men punted themselves out in a tub, to reach the places they had to open. Next morning the cellar looked like the scene of a shipwreck – all the barrels displaced, some floating and some sunk. The water drained off in time, but the hall and the two parlours retained so much dampness that we never lived downstairs again, and had all our meals brought up to the study."

The next Austen to become rector of Steventon was James's younger brother Henry, who had taken Holy Orders late in life following the failure of his banking partnership in London in 1816. Henry was determined to rebuild his life and in no position to argue about the dampness of the parsonage, and took over immediately in 1820 as soon as James's family had left. He only stayed for three years, until his nephew William Knight, one of Edward Knight's younger sons, was of an age to be ordained; William became rector in 1823 and stayed until his death in 1873, the second-longest serving rector Steventon has ever had.

Although Edward Knight seems to have been content that his brothers should live in a damp old parsonage, for his son he was prepared to incur the expenses of modernisation, and so in 1823-24 built a totally new rectory on the hillside opposite the old one. Once this was complete, the old house was demolished – its rubble was visible in the field for many years afterwards – and William Knight and his successors for the next century enjoyed the comforts of an architect-designed house standing in its own 56 acres of additional glebe land. During his incumbency William replaced the spire on the church, and also accepted the gift of a new font from the Digweed family. He reported to the Bishop of Winchester's religious census of Hampshire: "Church can hold up to 150 people. 1st March 1851: Morning service 32 plus 15 Sunday school, evening service 51 plus 16 Sunday school."

William Knight was the last member of the Austen family to serve the parish of Steventon – a total of 119 years since Thomas Bathurst's appointment as curate. The Duke of Wellington, having acquired the manor and its rights, sold the advowson to the Alder family, and the Revd Herbert Alder succeeded William Knight in 1874. His brother, the Revd Edward Alder, was rector from 1889-1901, and the latter's widow Mrs Naomi Alder sold the advowson in 1931 to the Martyrs' Memorial Trust, who relinquished their right of patronage to the Bishop of Winchester in 1972. However, in 1928 the parish of Steventon was united with that of North Waltham, and in 1930 the Revd Charles Rome Hall became the first rector of the two benefices, with his rectory at North Waltham. The Steventon rectory was therefore sold off into private ownership, and is now known as Steventon House. When it was up for sale in 2000, the agents described it as being a five-bedroomed Grade II Listed house, with gardens and grounds of 14 acres that included woodland, parkland, pasture, walled garden, staff cottage, stable block, tennis court and swimming pool.

Not much personal detail seems to be remembered about the rectors of the later nineteenth and early twentieth centuries. Henry Chandler, who came after Herbert Alder, erected a stained glass window in the church in 1887 as a thanksgiving for his life being preserved through a long and dangerous illness, but sadly spoke too soon, for he died the following year. In 1901, the census shows that the Revd Edward Alder had a family of seven young daughters living in the rectory, with probably one or two sons away at school in addition; and as it was noticed in the 1930s that a number of little garden-plots bordered by box edgings still existed in the grounds of Steventon House, perhaps these had been laid out for the Alder children's benefit.

In 1960 the parish of Dummer was joined to Steventon and North Waltham; and then in 1972 another arrangement was made – Dummer was joined to Ellisfield and Farleigh Wallop, and a new United Benefice was created of St Michael North Waltham, St Nicholas Steventon, Holy Trinity

& St Andrew Ashe, and All Saints Deane, with the Revd Basil Norris as its first rector. His immediate successor was the Revd Geoffrey Turner, a much travelled man, who had been in the Indian Army and the colonial police force before taking Holy Orders in later life.

The village and its inhabitants; the parish registers and census returns

Steventon at Domesday-time was probably no more than a few hovels of wattle and daub and thatch, huddled around the church and the manor house, and getting its necessary water supply from the springs which broke out between the layers of clay and gravel as the land sloped down to what is now the North Waltham lane. The first time any villager is mentioned by name is in 1249, when the joint lords of the manor Manser de Sandervill and Hugh de Wengham granted to William son of Robert of Steventon the right to take timber, underwood and bracken from their woodland, for use in building, repairing fences, and as fuel. This William might even be one and the same as William le Newman who in 1261 was charged with robbing the church of Steventon and then breaking out of the prison at Basingstoke; he was sentenced to be hanged, but escaped by the breaking of the cord – which in those days would have been seen as God's intervention to prove his innocence.

Basingstoke plays an important part in Steventon's history, as it was the chief town in the district and so the place where the Hundred Court – something like our modern magistrates' court – met every few weeks to dispense local justice. The villagers had to choose from amongst themselves a senior and reliable man – one for every ten families, and so called a tithingman – who would be their spokesman in all public affairs, and who was also something like a parish constable, responsible for keeping law and order in the village. One of the Steventon tithingman's tasks was to attend these Hundred Court sittings at Basingstoke, report any problems in the village, and take back the Court's ruling on the matter. The records of the court were written down in Court Rolls, and Basingstoke is lucky in that a number of these Rolls have survived, covering the years 1386-1700, and are now kept in the Hampshire Record Office in Winchester. For anyone with the time to read through them all, many names of early Steventonians would no doubt come to light; when the local scholars Francis Baigent and James Millard wrote their *History of the Ancient Town and Manor of Basingstoke* in 1889, they picked out some extracts from the Court Rolls as examples of the information to be found, and a few of those relating to Steventon are given below (with the wording largely modernised):

19th *April 1399*: the Steventon tithingman came with his friends and paid four shillings towards the Court's expenses. He reported that John Levers junior, John Pykamour and Nicholas Barell had each made two unlicensed brewings of ale; they were found guilty and fined sixpence each.

17th *November 1464*: the tithingman reported that John Cobbe and John Logeys had not yet joined any of the tithing groups; they now came and were sworn in to behave as peaceful and law-abiding citizens.

23rd *April 1485*: a black ram, worth sixpence, had been found astray in Steventon last Michaelmas and no-one had claimed it; agreed it could remain in the custody of Henry Smyth.

26th *April 1561*: the village was ordered to provide stocks, fit for the punishment of malefactors and vagabonds according to the law, within the next four weeks, or be fined six shillings and eightpence. (It is believed in Steventon today that these stocks were erected at The Triangle and were not removed until about 1845.)

Basingstoke's position on a main road, and as Steventon's nearest market town, was not always advantageous to the village. In 1348 the Black Death arrived in England, brought by merchant ships sailing from the Mediterranean to land their goods at Weymouth, and the infection spread rapidly up the roads towards London. It has been estimated that at least one-third of the population of England died within a year or two, and Basingstoke was one of the places devastated by the plague – three of its vicars were appointed and died between 1349-51. It seems likely that the infection was taken back to Steventon, perhaps by these very tithingmen who were attending the Hundred Courts, for there is likewise a long gap at this period in the records of rectors being appointed to the parish. The skeleton found beneath the Brocas manor house five hundred years later may have been one of the plague victims; and perhaps it was this calamity which led the survivors to abandon the desolated old village and build their cottages anew in the valley below, each side of the North Waltham lane and spreading westwards into what is now Steventon Lane and the present site of the modern village.

As well as the Basingstoke Court Rolls, the Hampshire Record Office also holds a number of original wills made by inhabitants of Steventon, the earliest of which is that of Christopher Denby, who died in 1528. From his will it can be seen that Denby was a pious and wealthy sheep-farmer, who was able to leave bequests in cash and kind not only to Steventon church, for maintaining lights before the altars, but also to Winchester Cathedral and the churches of Worting and Deane. Three of his children received 60 sheep apiece, a married daughter received 22 sheep, and all other members of his family were to have three sheep each – which still left plenty in hand for his widow to pay his outstanding debts to his neighbours totalling £6 and have enough to live on herself. Another four wills, written between 1533-35, link the families of Smythe and Wayte, who likewise left sheep to their kinsfolk, though not in the large numbers that Christopher Denby could command. Once the new régime of Henry VIII's Reformation takes effect in the middle of the sixteenth century, there are no more bequests in later wills to pay for lights before images in the church, or for masses to be said for the souls of the departed.

The parish registers start in 1604, and gradually their records of baptisms, marriages and burials link together with official taxation listings, estate documents and personal wills, to enable us to build up some pictures of the families who lived and farmed in Steventon in past years. The earliest records in the registers are often scanty and haphazard, but here and there sad little personal histories can be guessed at, lying behind the terse scrawl of the parson or his semi-literate parish clerk: "Agnes, surname unknown, servant to Sir Pexall Brocas, buried 3 December 1611." Was poor Agnes so old or so half-witted, that she could not remember her name? Or, indeed, had she ever had a surname? – was she an unwanted bastard left in a barn and given shelter in the manor house in return for her work? Someone else, years later, was so ashamed of bringing a bastard into the world that he or she managed to destroy part of the entry in the register: "[name scratched out] daughter of James [name scratched out] baptised 2 May 1655." Then there were the homeless wanderers: "John Newman, a vagrant person who was brought sick to the parish was buried ye first of December 1632" – "A vagrant maid coming sick to the parish not able to declare her name was buried the xixth [19th] of January AD 1632/3" – and the domestic tragedies: "The two daughters of George Passion being born dead were buried ye ixth [9th] day of June 1624" – "A Childe of Joseph Wheatly & Sarah his wife was borne Febr. 22nd 1704/5, wch. Childe died suddenly & so (to ye great grife of ye parents) unbaptised." The family of Passion/Pashon/ Patience appear in the registers during the seventeenth and early eighteenth centuries, and their name remains attached to the land they farmed – Patience Close appears on modern maps of Steventon, as also does Wheatleys Close.

In 1662 the Hearth Tax was introduced – which was then a new idea, being based not on individuals (a poll tax) but on the size of the house they occupied, as defined by the number of hearths or ovens it contained. Each hearth was taxed at two shillings p.a., but the very poorest householders were exempted. In Steventon, Sir John Lewkenor at the Manor House paid for ten hearths and the Revd John Orpwood at the rectory for three. There were two farmers who lived in better style than the parson – Thomas Small had five hearths and John Brothers four. William Patience, Michael Noyse and Charles Coney each had two hearths, Arthur Crooke, Austen Ansell, Richard Smart, John Philipps and William White had only one apiece; and the three poorest inhabitants, James Duthman, Thomas Fronknell, and the Widow Dounce, were listed as excused payment. The Hearth Tax proved very unpopular – presumably because it was more difficult to dodge than a poll tax would have been – and it was abolished in 1690 when William and Mary came to the throne.

From 1600 onwards more and more documents survive that provide information about the village and its inhabitants, though as yet many have still not been studied or transcribed. Apart from the Basingstoke Court Rolls, the Hampshire Record Office has another similar series, a long run of Steventon Manor Court Rolls from 1614-1764. These Manor Courts were local meetings for the villagers, usually chaired by the estate steward, and were the occasions when tenancies and rents were rearranged, or minor nuisances discussed and resolved. In the 1720s the Bassett family are first mentioned in these Rolls, when Richard and (probably) his brother John come to Steventon and take sub-tenancies of a house and some lands to the west of Steventon Lane; the family does not seem to have stayed in the parish for more than forty years, but somehow their name became attached to the area of their tenancies, first as Bassett's Buildings and then as Bassett's Farm, which remains so called to the present day.

Once the Revd George Austen and his family take up residence in Steventon rectory in 1768, their letters and later memoirs provide much more detailed and personal information about the village and its inhabitants during the second half of the eighteenth century. Mrs Austen had eight children in all, and it was her custom to nurse her babies herself for their first three months of life, then wean them and pass them out to foster-parents in the village to see them through the messy stages of infancy and toddler-hood until such time as they were fit to be brought back into the family circle. As her grandson James-Edward Austen-Leigh recalled, the infant was daily visited by one or both of its parents, and frequently brought to them at the parsonage, but the cottage was its home, and remained so till it was old enough to run about and talk. The large Littleworth family seems to have been Mrs Austen's choice for fostering, and they remained faithful servants and friends of the Austens for decades. Apart from their own children, there were also for many years three or four teenage boys at a time living in the rectory – Mr Austen's pupils, whom he tutored for entry into Oxford University, and who provided companionship for his sons in their studies and added something to the family income – and Mrs Austen had to be a surrogate mother to these boys as well. Another of her domestic tasks was to manage a small herd of Channel Island dairy cattle, and a poultry-yard where she bred turkeys, ducks and chickens to feed this large family group.

In 1754 the first officially printed register for the recording of banns and marriages came into use in the Church of England, in order to bring some regularity into the casual and frequently inadequate entries made by careless parsons or clerks. At the beginning of the volume there is a page showing three specimen entries – the correct wording, with blanks left where personal names and dates were to be inserted – for the calling of banns, the certificate of marriage, and the signatures of the couple concerned, together with those of their witnesses. Perhaps Mr Austen kept the registers at home rather than in the church, because at some time in

The Form of an Entry of Publication of Banns.

The Banns of Marriage between *A. B.* of *Henry Frederick Howard Fitzwilliam*

and *C. D.* of *Steventon* were duly publifhed in this

Church for the ⎰ firft ⎱
⎱ fecond ⎰ Time, on Sunday the
⎰ third ⎱

Day of in the Year One Thoufand Seven

Hundred and

J. J. Rector ⎱
Vicar ⎰
Curate ⎰

The Form of an Entry of a Marriage.

Edmund Arthur William Mortimer

A. B. of *Liverpool* and *C. D.* of *Steventon* *Jane Austen*

were married in this Church by ⎰ Banns ⎱ this
⎱ Licenfe* ⎰

Day of in the Year One Thoufand Seven

Hundred and by me

J. J. Rector ⎱
Vicar ⎰
Curate ⎰

This Marriage was folemnized between us *A. B. C. B.* late *C. D.*

in the Prefence of *E. F. G. H.* *Jack Smith, Jno. Smith*

---

* Infert thefe Words, viz. *with Confent of* ⎰ *Parents* ⎱ where both, or either
⎱ *Guardians* ⎰

of the Parties to be married *by Licenfe*, are under Age.

---

12. Jane Austen's mock entries in the Steventon Marriage register, by kind
permission of Hampshire Record Office (71M82/PR3)

her teens Jane was able to lay hands on the marriage register and could not resist filling in these blank spaces with the elegant names of imaginary suitors:

"The Banns of Marriage between *Henry Frederic Howard Fitzwilliam* of *London* and *Jane Austen* of *Steventon* were duly published in this Church ....." followed by:

"*Edmund Arthur William Mortimer* of *Liverpool* and *Jane Austen* of *Steventon* were married in this Church by Banns ..." but then prosaic reality took over:

"This Marriage was solemnized between us *Jack Smith, Jane Smith late Austen,* in the Presence of *Jack Smith, Jane Smith.*"

Jane's elder brother Henry was officially witness to a wedding in 1779, even though he was only eight at the time; Jane and Cassandra witnessed their cousin Jane Cooper's wedding to Captain Sir Thomas Williams in 1792; and on some occasions Jane herself wrote the entries in the registers: the baptisms of Charlotte Littleworth in 1791 and of Ann Martel in 1792, the marriage of Joseph Barley and Mary Wilkins in 1800, and the sadder event of the burial of Nathaniel Martell junior in March 1801 – a boy who was 'kill'd by a Waggon going over him' – presumably because no parish clerk was then available to undertake the task.

Jane's surviving letters to her sister Cassandra start in 1796, and before she and her parents left Steventon in the spring of 1801 there are several mentions of the rectory servants and of some of the other villagers. Anne ('Nanny') Littleworth was the Austens' cook, her husband John was the groom/coachman, and their eldest daughter Eliza-Jane, baptised on 29th October 1789, was Jane's god-daughter. Anne ('Nanny') Hilliard was housekeeper/ladies-maid – when she was ill the Austens had to employ two charwomen to do the heavier work, which was inconvenient, and Nanny Littleworth had to be asked to 'dress' Jane's hair – a situation which she knew Cassandra would find amusing. Nanny Hilliard and her husband had an idea they would like to become innkeepers, and Mr Austen wrote on their behalf to the local brewers to try to find a place for them, possibly at Farnham when the next vacancy occurred there – but in January 1801 Nanny was still working at the rectory, so perhaps the Hilliards changed their minds. John Bond was the bailiff who managed the glebe-land farm for Mr Austen, and his daughter Lizzie was later on apprenticed to a local dressmaker.

Apart from these full-time employees, Dame Bushell was the Austens' washerwoman, and when she retired in 1798 her replacement was John Steevens' wife, about whom Jane commented doubtfully: "She does not look as if anything she touched would ever be clean, but who knows?"

Dame Staples was temporarily a maidservant until a young girl was engaged at the end of 1798: "We are very much disposed to like our new maid; she knows nothing of a dairy, to be sure, which, in our family, is rather against her, but she is to be taught it all. … As yet, she seems to cook very well, is uncommonly stout [sturdy] and says she can work well at her needle."

Jane and Cassandra were accustomed to visit their father's older and poorer parishioners, and when Cassandra was away from home on one occasion Jane wrote that she had called on Betty Lovell, "who enquired particularly after you, and said she seemed to miss you very much, because you used to call in upon her very often. This was an oblique reproach at me, which I am sorry to have merited, and from which I will profit." As the squire of Steventon, Edward Knight sent money to pay for winter presents for the most needy of the villagers – in 1798 Jane was buying worsted stockings for Mary Hutchins, Dame Kew, Mary Steevens, Dame Staples, a shift for Hannah Staples and a shawl for Betty Dawkins. In 1800 she bought ten pairs of worsted stockings, and a shift – "The shift is for Betty Dawkins, as we find she wants it more than a rug – she is one of the most grateful of all whom Edward's charity has reached, or at least she expresses herself more warmly than the rest, for she sends him a 'sight of thanks'".

In 1798, when there was the likelihood of a French invasion, the Government sent out a questionnaire under the Defence of the Realm Act to check on the state of preparedness of the Hampshire countryside. Daniel Smallbone the tithingman of Steventon compiled the required returns, which give us another snapshot of the parish just at the turn of the century: there were 39 able-bodied men and 10 infirm incapable men; no-one was serving in the volunteer militia; no foreigners; no Quakers; and 78 non-combatants who would need help to be evacuated. Live and dead stock amounted to 5 cows, 1100 sheep and goats, 64 pigs, 4 riding horses and

34 draft horses; 12 wagons, 5 carts; 20 ovens which could be used to bake regular supplies of bread; 380 quarters of wheat, 250 quarters of oats, 200 quarters of barley, 220 loads of hay, 10 loads of straw, 50 quarters of vetches, 1 threshing machine (that was the big one up at the Manor House). Thirty men were prepared to fight on foot and five on horseback, but they had no military weapons, only their agricultural tools – axes, spades, shovels, billhooks and saws; the remaining four men would act as guides or servants. Luckily, as in 1940, the danger passed off, and after another similar scare in 1804, Nelson's victory at Trafalgar in 1805 meant it was no longer possible for Napoleon to contemplate a cross-Channel invasion of England.

The next official requirement was in 1801, when in the wake of the food shortages of 1800 the Government instructed country clergymen to report on the crops being cultivated in their parishes, and Mr Austen replied that Steventon had 267 acres wheat, 250 acres barley, 250 acres oats, 60 acres turnips or rape, 28 acres rye, 12 acres peas, and 1½ acres potatoes. These political worries may have encouraged Mr Austen to retire from his parochial duties, and in 1801 he and his wife and daughters went to Bath, where he died in 1805.

James Austen now became curate of Steventon, and succeeded as rector following his father's death. James enjoyed writing poetry to while away the long winter evenings, and gave a pen-picture of the village: the bare downland with its grazing sheep, small copses with oak, elm, ash, maple and sycamore trees, and green meadows bounded by thorn hedges; the well-kept whitewashed cottages had grape-vines and woodbine clinging to their walls, and their gardens grew beans, colewort and potatoes. His son James-Edward remembered that the cottagers' wives sat at home spinning flax and wool. James's elder daughter Anna had clear memories of the cottagers themselves, and many years later wrote:

"Why should I pass over without notice our poorer neighbours, though unknown to fame – save in the instance of Bet Littleworth, whose exploits tradition may still preserve in her native village; whilst few or none remember Dame Staples with her pleasant face, and tidy cottage, or her sluttish nextdoor neighbour Betty Dawkins, with her sheepish, half-witted ragged husband, Phil – nor the school mistress, with flattened bonnet approaching to a bonnegrace [a shady hat worn by country-women], an elderly woman but still called young Dame Tilbury to distinguish her from an older dowager of that name. Nor testy old Will Littleworth, known by the name of 'Uncle Will', still less the individual called 'Shepherd' ... [though that was not] his real name. Always at leisure to assist by his presence in the cutting up of our bacon pigs, guessing at their weight, comparing past with present; and though I know not if I ever actually saw him doing anything, he was no doubt an important person in the parish.

"Then there was Henny Lavender, who had been a beauty, the admired of my grandfather's elder pupils and late in life changed her fancy-sounding name for Dry – so neat, so clean and industrious, so discontented and dissatisfied – it was almost a treat to listen to her grumblings or a vexation, as the case might be. Hating, after our removal, the new parsonage, its new inmates, and their new ways with a deadly hatred, though whilst we staid it was very hard indeed to win a smile of approbation. However, though no beauty, Bet Littleworth was our heroine – though a rather small and delicate-looking woman, she had all her life by choice done the work of a man. She went on errands, once travelled on foot from Steventon to Godmersham, more than a hundred miles. It was her delight in after life to relate the history of that adventure, and how the Squire came out to welcome her arrival, and gave a special charge to his servants to make much of her because she was his old playfellow. Bet worked too in the fields or as an occasional gardener and by degrees came to rent a few acres on her own account, became the owner of a donkey and a cart and finally of a cow. She had for many years a suitor – perhaps for the greater part of her life – he came occasionally of a Sunday to visit her from some neighbouring village, but they were never married. Bet in utter disregard of pastoral admonitions or parochial efforts for the suppression of vice, preferred spending her strength and earnings in the maintenance of the two illegitimate children of a niece. A very dissipated character was that niece, Bet Armstrong with her plausible and almost pleasant manner but she seldom came amongst us. All these and many others have passed away, and their place knows them no more, nor in good truth could they return would they know the place. Cottages and gardens, the homes of some have disappeared, the first pulled down and the last enclosed, whilst all would miss the village playground, and the old maple tree beneath which they congregated on Sunday afternoons."

Most of the people Anna mentions can be traced in the parish registers – in addition, Mrs James Austen made a specific note in her diary that Betty Dawkins was buried on 16th April 1810, so perhaps she was glad to see the last of this unsatisfactory member of the community. The village playground to which Anna refers seems to have been the area now known as The Triangle.

In 1808 a fire broke out one March night in the two cottages close to the rectory; bailiff John Bond rushed to save a horse in the adjacent stable, but while he was doing so his house was gutted, so James Austen gave him and his wife rooms in the rectory for their future home. Poor old Betty Lovell, in the other cottage, survived for a day or two, but the register records her burial on 9th March – 'died in consequence of the fire which took place at the house where she lived'.

Some happier events have also been recorded: 1809 was the Golden Jubilee of George III's Coronation, and the occasion was loyally marked by civic celebrations and private parties throughout the land; at Steventon James Austen and the Digweeds at the Manor House organised a dinner for the parish in the Digweeds' barn. A few years later, one of James-Edward's school-friends, 12-year-old William Heathcote (later to become Sir William Heathcote, 5th baronet, of Hursley Park), stayed at Steventon rectory during the summer holidays, and on 19th July 1813 wrote a vivid letter to his cousin Margaret Blackstone, describing the

".... merry-making at Steventon, which Mr. Digweed gave (on Saturday evening) to his haymakers, when all his hay was got in. There were donkey races, merely for the sport, old women in wheel-barrows blindfolded, for two blue ribbon bows, young women to run a race for a straw bonnet, girls for two pink ribbons, boys to run in sacks for harvest gloves not bugs, to roll down an hill for a plum pudding, to run a race for a handkerchief, & lastly to dip their heads into a bucket of water for some oranges. I got a donkey lent me to run (the one I used to ride), [James] Edward Austen was my jockey, he was dressed in this manner, he had a black velvet cap, with a yellow button on the top, & a yellow band in front, & buff coat with black sleeves, we managed that in this manner, first he put on a black velvet spencer of Mrs. Austen's, & over that, a buff waistcoat, it looked very well I assure you. I think you would be quite amused to see the old women wheel their barrows, in one part of the field there was a rake, to which the prizes were hung, which was the goal, & another stick for the starting post, they did not run a race all at the same time, as perhaps you suppose, but one at a time & they (not seeing the goal) but [to] go on as long as they liked & stop whenever they thought they were near the end of their journey, so that some women, by letting one hand lower than the other might turn their barrows completely round thinking that they were as straight as any of them all the time, when all had all done they measured the distance of each woman's barrow from the goal, & that one which was nearest obtained the prize."

During William Knight's long incumbency, he did much to improve living conditions in the village; the little whitewashed creeper-smothered cottages, which James Austen viewed with a poetic eye, were in fact damp, dark and over-crowded, and William made it clear to his father Edward Knight that new housing was urgently needed. As a start, in the 1820s William built several cottages at the north end of Steventon Lane and gave the freeholds to the villagers who were living in the valley between William's own new rectory and the site of the old one; Jane Austen's god-daughter Eliza-Jane Littleworth and her husband George Church were one of the first families to move into the new houses, and thereafter the old ones were cleared away and their sites turned into meadow-land, as Anna recalled. Other cottages, substantially constructed of brick or flints with slate roofs, were built in the 1830s, the group at Stonehills followed in the 1860s, and Mr Harris erected still more in the 1880s and '90s. As a result, probably the only surviving houses which Jane Austen would have seen are The Forge near the railway, Elm Tree Cottage at The Triangle, Jasmine Cottage (at one time a smithy), Yew Tree Cottage and the old Bassetts farmhouse in Steventon Lane, and perhaps the two Hatch Gate cottages at the cross-roads south of the village.

'Cottages now pulled down' – a drawing made in the middle of the nineteenth century

The railway came to Hampshire in 1839-40, when the line from London to Southampton was laid out via Basingstoke and crossed the north-west corner of Steventon parish; the first through train to Southampton ran on 11th May 1840. There had been a suggestion that a station might be built at Steventon, but it seems that the Knight family objected, so instead it was sited at Micheldever and was then called the Andover Road station. The running of the first train was celebrated at Micheldever by a barbecue, when a whole ox was roasted, and part of the meat was brought back to Steventon and eaten by the villagers at a party in Northdown Field. These early trains were very slow, and the passengers paying the cheapest fares had to sit in open-top carriages and shelter themselves as best they could beneath umbrellas when the weather was bad. So slow was the rate of travel, indeed, that the Steventon village boys could play a wicked joke on the passengers, by holding up bunches of wild-flowers for them to grab as they trundled by, and which they discovered too late included very prickly thistles. Within a few years the cottages at Stonehills were occupied by railway staff – plate-layers and signalmen – as it was most convenient for them just to walk up the embankment behind their homes and so on along the railway line to Micheldever in one direction, Church Oakley or Basingstoke in the other. When travelling today between London and Winchester, it is possible to look down as the train passes along the embankment and catch a glimpse of these Stonehills cottages and those of the 1820s opposite, but the speed is now such that the view is no sooner recognised than left behind.

It was in 1801 that the Government decided to hold a census every ten years, but unfortunately the complete returns for the decades before 1841 were not preserved once the basic figures had been published as 'Population Abstracts'. The first census shows that Steventon had 153 inhabitants, and this number gradually increased during the nineteenth century to a high point of 288 in 1881, but dropping back thereafter to 229 in 1901. Thanks to computerisation and the internet it is now possible to read each census from 1841 up to and including 1901, and to trace how the inhabitants and their occupations have changed down the years. There was always a blacksmith working in the village, and the Church family were useful tradesmen – grocer, baker, and carpenters. There were always some shepherds, from three in 1851 up to a maximum of seven in 1871, but thereafter dropping back to four at the end of the century. The first cowman or herdsman appears in 1881, and their numbers and presumably their herds increase just as the shepherds and their flocks decrease. Most of the men were described simply as 'agricultural labourer', with 'carter' being a more specific occupation.

Early in the century 'young Dame Tilbury' was responsible for teaching the children the elements of the Three Rs, and presumably other village wives maintained the dame-school after her, for it is not until 1861 that the first professional school mistress appears; and even then, her premises could not have been large, for some children went to a school at North Waltham, until Mr Harris built Steventon's own school in 1893, staffed by two teachers. This school was taken over by Hampshire County Council in 1903 and closed in 1964, since when the children have gone again to North Waltham for their primary education and the 'Old School House' has become a private home.

From about the 1850s until the 1870s English agriculture enjoyed a golden age of prosperity, with high productivity going in tandem with expanding markets. Steam power was applied to farm machinery, and on large farms stationary traction engines were used for threshing, baling, and to some extent ploughing as well – in 1881 there were three men in Steventon who gave their occupation to the census enumerator as 'engine-driver'. The Digweed family at the Manor House had their share of this prosperity – in 1871 they were farming 1380 acres and employing 39 men and seven boys, practically all the male workers in the village. After 1875 prices fell and a depression quickly followed, made worse by bad weather and poor harvests and imports of cheap grain from the newly-cultivated prairies of North America. As the railway network was extended westwards beyond Southampton, immigrants came to Steventon: in 1891 a little colony of Dorset-born workers settled at Cheesedown, when John Henry Fooks, the tenant farmer, brought with him his own employees and their families, Joseph Leaves the carter and Levi Lane the herdsman.

The changes made by Mr Harris during his ownership of the estate are likewise reflected in the censuses: in 1881 the village was full of lodgers – ten plasterers and twelve joiners – and a 'machinist' at Peak Hill House employing six men. These men were obviously working on the internal fitting-out of the new Manor House; and the two bricklayers also shown were probably engaged upon building new cottages. Two farm stewards were employed, one Scottish and one from Norfolk, based at Warren Farm and Bassetts Farm respectively, to run the estate in the absence of the new owner. When the Harris family took up residence, they brought with them a houseful of servants who came from all over the south of England and beyond – the parlour maid had been born in Malta, and the lady's-maid came from North Germany – and later on they employed a Swiss couple as butler and cook.

In the 1860s Jane Austen's nephew James-Edward began collecting information with a view to writing her biography, and in 1869 stayed with his cousin William Knight for a few days to re-visit the site of his boyhood home in the old rectory. He wrote to his sister Anna: "All traces of former things are even more obliterated than I had expected. .... they have discovered and opened an old well, which must have been in our grandfather's old garden, between the house & the terrace; did you know of any such? " Anna replied: "You asked me about the existence of a well ... to be sure there was, and as it remained for some time only covered over I rather wonder that you do not remember it also. It was originally in the square walled-in cucumber garden. Somewhere I think about the centre. The walls of this inner garden were covered with cherry and other fruit trees ... I remember this sunny cucumber garden – its frames, and also its abundance of pot-herbs, marigolds, etc ..."

James-Edward's *A Memoir of Jane Austen* was published in 1870; although quite short, it was nevertheless the first proper biography of Jane, and brought Steventon to the notice of the outside world as her birthplace. In 1884 another member of the family, Lord Brabourne, one of Jane's great-nephews, published the first collection of her letters, and these two books between them started a trickle of visitors to the village, which is now nearly turning into a flood. The first literary pilgrim seems to have been the American Oscar Fay Adams, from Boston, who came to England in 1889 and took some photographs, which are probably the earliest surviving pictures of the places Jane knew. He noticed the modern rectory, "a cheerful two-storeyed mansion, at the top of a well-kept, sunny

THE SITE OF THE OLD PARSONAGE, STEVENTON

14. The site of the old rectory – drawing by Ellen Hill, 1900

lawn," and that south of the sloping lawn was ..."a small field, shaded at one end by large elms. A disused pump here, and a depression which must once have been a cellar, are now all the signs remaining to mark the spot where the rectory of Steventon stood, seventy years ago."

Then in the summer of 1900 the writer Constance Hill, accompanied by her artist sister Ellen to draw the illustrations, came down from London to gain local colour for Constance's forthcoming biography of Jane; the sisters spent a night at the Deane Gate Inn, and trotted down in a pony chaise to Steventon early the next morning. After passing through the dark narrow tunnel underneath the railway, known as Steventon Arch, they came to the 1820s cottages on the east side of Steventon Lane, and stopped at the first one to talk to "an old man leaning on his garden gate" who turned out to be John Church, son of Jane's god-daughter Eliza-Jane Littleworth; he told them of this connection, and that his Littleworth grandfather had been coachman to James Austen. He gave the Hills directions to identify the site of the old rectory, and added that the pump in the middle of the field had a well underneath it, and was originally in the wash-house at the back of the parsonage. He remembered the old parsonage being pulled down in the 1820s and "all the bricks and rubbish lying about on the ground."

In 1903 a lamplighter was appointed by the parish council to light the lamps in Steventon Arch; he was paid three shillings a week and had to provide the oil, glasses, and wicks himself. Even though mains electricity came to the village in 1938, it was not until the 1960s that electric lighting was installed in the tunnel itself. Mains water came in 1954, and before then the villagers had lived as their ancestors had done, relying upon wells, boreholes, or rainwater-butts.

Also in 1903 a Methodist meeting was formed, with their chapel in the corner of a field that was reached by a track leading off Steventon Lane. It was built of corrugated iron, with a wooden lining, lit by oil lamps and warmed by a smoky coke stove in winter, with music for the hymns provided by a small harmonium. The meetings continued until 1972, and the last stewards from 1950 onwards were Mr and Mrs Bertie Titheridge; they lived on the west side of the railway embankment and Mr Titheridge worked on the railway as a signalman. Mrs Titheridge organised a Sunday

School and women's group, while her husband also acted as churchwarden at St Nicholas's church.

Mr Henry Henshaw came to Steventon in 1928, to manage the estate as resident agent for the Onslow Fanes, and stayed until his death in 1960. He was interested in the history of the village, and recorded memories from the then oldest inhabitants Bertie Church (the son of the John Church who was proud of his mother's connection with Jane Austen) and Arthur Green, and wrote these down in the 1950s. Without his care, much local knowledge would otherwise have been lost – for example, these elderly residents were able to remember that at one time a concertina was used in church to lead off the hymn-singing before a harmonium was installed in 1875, this in turn making way for the Mills family's gift of the present organ in 1912. Mr Henshaw's daughter Mary played the organ for the church services, and as she was very lovely all the men in the congregation used to gaze at her. During the first half of the twentieth century there was still a gang of mummers based in North Waltham, who would call at Steventon Manor House to entertain the Christmas-party guests; one little girl who saw them in the 1930s remembered that they disguised themselves under hats covered with streamers made from long strips of wallpaper.

The village hall was built in the early 1930s on land that had once been part of Street Farm, owned and given by Mr Jack Onslow Fane. The Patience family had lived here in the seventeenth century, and when William Patience died in 1676 he was obviously a thriving farmer, for his inventory shows he had an eight-roomed house, a barn, plenty of stored grain, sheep, cows and pigs, amounting to a total value of £85.7s.10d. It is not known when this house was demolished, but some traces of old walls can still be seen around the modern buildings. The new hall was first known as the Steventon Church Room, and had a consecrated sanctuary at one end, included to encourage the residents to attend church services, as St Nicholas was so far out of the village; for this reason the then rector, Revd Charles Rome Hall, disapproved of any form of entertainment being held there. It became the Parish Hall in 1976, when the sanctuary was de-consecrated and the building was leased to a management committee representing all community interests in the village.

It seems Steventon has never had an inn, either because the villagers were happy to brew their own ale and beer, or because such a development was forbidden by the Knight family. In 1737 old Madam Knight gave permission to her tenant William Brown to build a house at the crossroads on the waste of Steventon (now known as Hatch Gate), but "to be obledged never to make it a publick house or to sell Wine Beer or any Spiritous Liquors"; when William Brown died in 1754 Mr Thomas Knight bought the house from his widow and agreed that she and her six children could live on in one half of it, at a rent of one shilling a year, but again with the proviso she was not to sell "any Beer Wine Brandy or any other Liquor whatsoever." Later owners of the estate took a more relaxed view, for the 1851 and 1861 censuses show a Mary Taylor as being a beer-seller, likewise the Church family in 1891 and 1901, but the nearest inn proper was always that at Deane Gate on the main road. In the middle of the last century Bertie Church's cottage was used as an off-licence and general stores, and later as a Post Office and shop called Lytle House, after its then owner, but reverted to being a private residence in 1978.

In 1932 the Oxford scholar Dr R.W. Chapman published a more comprehensive collection of Jane Austen's letters, and also prepared the first really scholarly edition of her novels, which together put Steventon well and truly on the map of English literature. Miss Emma Austen-Leigh (granddaughter of James-Edward) put up the plaque to Jane in the church in 1936, and the following year wrote a little guidebook for the benefit of the visitors who were now becoming a regular feature of life in the village. Since then, there have been numerous biographies of Jane, and many television or film adaptations of her novels, the appearance of each of which encourages another wave of visitors, both to Steventon to see the place where she grew up and first started to write, to Chawton to see the place where she lived at the end of her life and wrote her later novels, and to Winchester to see her grave in the Cathedral. In July 1975 Steventon organised a week-long festival, with special church services, music, games and dancing, to celebrate the bicentenary of her birth, and later in the year the Post Office issued a set of commemorative stamps and first-day covers. These first-day covers were taken in style by a coach and four horses from the Steventon village hall to the Beach Arms inn at Oakley, and many residents along the route turned out to watch. The next date to commemorate will be 2017, the bicentenary of Jane's death, and no doubt Steventon will be happy to arrange another festival and receive the visitors who will come to join in the events.

None of the other Steventon inhabitants, past or present, has ever had such fame as that which now glows around the memory of Jane Austen; but as a Victorian author wrote: "… the growing good of the world is partly dependent on unhistorical acts; and that things are not so ill with you and me as they might have been, is half owing to the number who lived faithfully a hidden life, and rest in unvisited tombs."

RECTORS OF STEVENTON

from		to
before 1301	Geoffrey de Monteney	after 1305
1307	Roger des Roches	after 1308
1324	John de Pulburgh	?
before 1346	Thomas de Insula	resigns 1348
1349	Geoffrey [or Walter] de Brokhampton	?
?	John Chitterne	resigns 1375
1376	John Depynge	exchanges 1381 with
	Robert de Haytefelde from Hertford	?
1396	John Chitterne	resigns 1399
1399	John Stevenes	resigns 1401
1401	Roland de Thornburgh	resigns 1404
1404	Richard Scarburghe	resigns 1405
1405	Richard Gerard	resigns 1409
1409	John Colet	?
?	John Speny	resigns 1451
1451	John Baron	dies 1467
1468	Thomas Herryson	dies 1472
1472	John Marflete	dies 1481
1482	Robert Fawley	?
before 1517	John Wafer	dies 1538
1538	John Bennett	after 1545
after 1551	Richard Mills	dies 1581
1582	Ralph Thompson	dies 1591
1591	Peter Sefton	resigns 1596
1596	John Browne	resigns 1599
1599	Henry Nelson	?
1602	John Orpwood	dies 1658
1661	John Orpwood junior	dies 1694
1695	Richard Deane	dies 1697
1697	Thomas Church	dies 1720
1721	Richard Wright	dies 1726

1727	John Church	dies 1733
1733	David Strahan	dies 1737
1737	Henry Haddon	dies 1743
1743	William Payne	resigns 1751
1751	Stephen Apthorp	resigns 1759
1759	Henry Austen	resigns 1761
1761	George Austen	dies 1805
1805	James Austen	dies 1819
1820	Henry Thomas Austen	resigns 1823
1823	William Knight	dies 1873
1874	Herbert Alder	resigns 1884
1886	Henry Chandler	dies 1888
1889	Edward Alder	dies 1901
1901	Herbert Steedman	resigns 1930

1930 Steventon benefice united with that of North Waltham

1930	Charles Rome Hall	resigns 1948
1948	Louis Arthur Bralant	resigns 1950
1950	Colin Joseph Thompson	resigns 1959

1960 Dummer benefice united with Steventon and North Waltham

1961	William Basil Norris	resigns 1976

1972 new United Benefice created: St Michael, North Waltham; St Nicholas, Steventon; Holy Trinity & St Andrew, Ashe; and All Saints, Deane. Dummer is joined to Ellisfield and Farleigh Wallop.

1976	Geoffrey Turner	resigns 1992
1992	Michael Kenning	

SOURCES

Victoria County History of Hampshire (London, 1910)

Oxford Dictionary of National Biography (Oxford, 2005)

The Archaeological Journal (London, 1849)

Proceedings of the Hampshire Field Club (Winchester, 1938-40, 1943)

Reports of the Jane Austen Society (Chawton, 1949 continuing)

Oscar Fay Adams, *The Story of Jane Austen's Life* (Boston, USA, 1897)

Emma Austen-Leigh, *Jane Austen and Steventon* (London, 1937)

James Edward Austen-Leigh, *A Memoir of Jane Austen* ... ed. Kathryn Sutherland (Oxford World's Classics, 2002)

R. A. Austen-Leigh, *Austen Papers 1704-1856* (London, 1942)

Francis Joseph Baigent and James Elwin Millard, *A History of ... Basingstoke* (Basingstoke and London, 1889)

Egerton Brydges, *The Autobiography .... of Sir Egerton Brydges* (London, 1834)

Richard Coates, *The Place-Names of Hampshire* (London, 1989)

Julian Evans, *What Happened to Our Wood* (Alton, 2002)

David J. Eveleigh, *The Victorian Farmer* (Princes Risborough, 1991)

David Hugh Farmer, *Oxford Dictionary of Saints* (Oxford, 1978)

Henry Henshaw, *Steventon Hampshire, Historical Notes and Anecdotes* (pamphlet written 1953, issued Steventon 1997 with updating notes)

L.F. Hewey, *The Story of North Waltham Hampshire,* local pamphlet, 1966

Constance Hill, *Jane Austen, her Homes and her Friends* (London, 1902, 1904)

Elizabeth Hughes and Philippa White, eds., *The Hampshire Hearth Tax Assessment 1665* (Winchester, 1991)

Deirdre Le Faye, *Jane Austen, a Family Record* (1989, revised and enlarged 2nd edn Cambridge, 2004)

ed., *Jane Austen's Letters* (Oxford, 1995, 1997)

ed., *Reminiscences of Jane Austen's Niece Caroline Austen* (Chawton, rev ed 2004)

John Morris, general editor: *Domesday Book (4) Hampshire,* ed. Julian Munby (Chichester 1982)

Nikolaus Pevsner, general editor, *The Buildings of England: London, I* (Harmondsworth, 1957)

—— —— and David Lloyd, *Hampshire and the Isle of Wight* (Harmondsworth, 1967 rep. 1990)

Kevin Robertson, *London and South Western Railway, 150 Years …* (Ledbury, 1988)

David Selwyn, ed., *The Complete Poems of James Austen …* (Chawton, 2003)

Dominic Tweddle, Martin Biddle, Birthe Kjolbye-Biddle et al, *Corpus of Anglo-Saxon Stone Sculpture*, IV, S.E. England (pubd for The British Academy by OUP, 1995)

Charles Vancouver, *General View of the Agriculture of Hampshire* (London, 1813)

John A. Vickers, ed., *The Religious Census of Hampshire 1851* (Winchester, 1993)

W.R. Ward, ed., *Parson and Parish in Eighteenth-Century Hampshire - Replies to Bishops' Visitations* (Winchester, 1995)

Rupert Willoughby, *Sherborne St John & The Vyne in the Time of Jane Austen* (privately published Sherborne St John, 2002)

Unpublished sources in Hampshire Record Office, Winchester:

Austen-Leigh archive, 23M93/

Bramston archive, 20M64/

Heathcote archive, 63M84/

Knight archive, 18M61/, 39M89/ and 79M78/

Winchester diocesan archives - Bishops' Registers or Act Books, 21M65/A1/ and Visitations 21M65/B1/

Wills of Steventon residents, 16th-19th centuries – various individual call-marks

Census returns 1841-1901 inclusive now available online.

Also published by the Jane Austen Society

Collected Reports 1949 – 1965
Collected Reports 1966 – 1975
Collected Reports 1976 – 1985
Collected Reports 1986 – 1995
Collected Reports 1996 – 2000
(includes index for 1949 – 2000)

Godmersham Park, by Nigel Nicolson
Jane Austen in Bath, by Jean Freeman
My Aunt, Jane Austen: a memoir, by Caroline Austen
Reminiscences of Caroline Austen, ed Deirdre Le Faye
Jane Austen in Lyme Regis, by Maggie Lane
Jane Austen's Family & Tonbridge by Margaret Wilson
Jane Austen: A Celebration ed Maggie Lane & David Selwyn
Fanny Knight's Diaries, ed Deirdre Le Faye
James Austen's Complete Poems, ed David Selwyn
Fugitive Pieces: The poems of James Edward Austen-Leigh
ed David Selwyn
Jane Austen and the North Atlantic ed Sarah Emsley
The Letters of Mrs Lefroy ed Helen Lefroy & Gavin Turner

In association with the Carcanet Press
Jane Austen: Collected Poems and Verse of the
Austen family, ed David Selwyn